FAMILY
BUSINESS
GROWTH TIPS
Technique for family business growth

By

JUDITH WALTER

TABLE OF CONTENTS

CHAPTER FOUR: Embrace Technology

4.1 Introduction

4.2 Importance of embracing technology

4.3 Improving efficiency and productivity

4.4 Enhancing customer experience

4.5 Streamlining communication and collaboration

4.6 Providing valuable data insights for informed decision-making

4.7 Choosing the right technology solutions

4.8 Providing training and support for employees

CHAPTER FIVE: Plan for Succession

5.1 Introduction

5.2 Importance of succession planning

5.3 Identifying potential successors

5.4 Developing a leadership development program

CHAPTER ONE

DEVELOP A CLEAR BUSINESS STRATEGY

In today's competitive business environment, developing a clear and effective business strategy is critical to the success of any company, including family businesses. A clear business strategy is the foundation for making informed decisions, setting goals and objectives, and implementing plans that will enable the business to grow and thrive.

Family businesses have unique challenges and opportunities when it comes to developing a business strategy. On one hand, family businesses benefit from a shared sense of purpose and long-term commitment, and often have strong relationships with their customers and communities. On the other hand, family businesses can face challenges such as managing relationships with family members, balancing personal and business goals, and ensuring that the business remains viable for future generations.

This chapter will provide practical tips and strategies for developing a clear business strategy for family businesses. It will outline the key components of a successful strategy, including conducting market research, identifying competitive advantages and unique selling points, setting measurable goals and objectives, and developing a plan for sustainable growth. Readers will learn how to develop a strategy that aligns with their family business values, goals, and strengths, and that can guide decision-making and help them navigate challenges and opportunities.

By the end of this chapter, readers will have a better understanding of the importance of a clear business strategy for family businesses, and how they can develop and implement a successful strategy to drive growth and sustainability.

IMPORTANCE OF A CLEAR BUSINESS STRATEGY

A clear business strategy is essential for the success of any company, including family businesses. A strategy provides direction and focus, guiding decision-making and ensuring that all business activities are aligned towards achieving the company's goals and objectives. In the context of family businesses, a clear strategy is even more critical, as it helps to manage relationships between family members and ensure that personal and business goals are aligned.

HERE ARE SOME OF THE KEY REASONS WHY A CLEAR BUSINESS STRATEGY IS SO IMPORTANT:

1.Provides clarity and direction: A clear strategy defines the company's vision, mission, values, and goals, providing clarity and direction for all stakeholders. This helps to ensure that everyone is on the same page, working towards the same objectives, and helps to avoid conflicts and misunderstandings.

2.Enables informed decision-making: A strategy provides a framework for decision-making, helping business owners and managers to evaluate options and make informed choices that are aligned with the company's goals and values. This ensures that all decisions are made with a clear understanding of their impact on the company's long-term success.

3.Helps to manage risks and opportunities: A clear strategy enables businesses to identify and manage risks and opportunities, ensuring that they are well-positioned to adapt to changing market conditions and take advantage of new opportunities as they arise.

4.Supports sustainable growth: A strategy provides a roadmap for sustainable growth, outlining the steps that need to be taken to achieve the company's long-term goals. This helps to ensure that the business remains viable and profitable over the long term.

5.Provides a competitive advantage: A clear strategy can provide a competitive advantage, enabling the business to differentiate itself from competitors and deliver unique value to customers. This can help to attract and retain customers, and ultimately drive growth and profitability.

In summary, a clear business strategy is essential for the success of any company, and particularly important for family businesses. It provides direction and focus, enables informed decision-making, helps to manage risks and opportunities, supports sustainable growth, and provides a competitive advantage. By developing and implementing a clear strategy, family businesses can navigate the challenges of managing relationships between family members and achieve long-term success.

KEY COMPONENTS OF A SUCCESSFUL BUSINESS STRATEGY

Conducting market research

One of the most critical components of a successful business strategy is conducting market research. Market research involves gathering information about the industry, target customers, and competitors to gain a deeper understanding of the market and identify opportunities for growth. This information can then be used to inform the development of a strategy that is tailored to the specific needs of the business and the market in which it operates.

HERE ARE SOME OF THE KEY BENEFITS OF CONDUCTING MARKET RESEARCH

1.Identifying customer needs: Market research helps businesses to identify the needs and preferences of their target customers, enabling them to develop products and services that are tailored to their specific needs.

2.Understanding the competition: Market research helps businesses to understand the strengths and weaknesses of their competitors, enabling them to develop strategies to differentiate themselves and gain a competitive advantage.

3.Identifying market trends: Market research helps businesses to identify trends in the market, such as changing customer preferences or emerging technologies, which can be leveraged to create new opportunities for growth.

4.Assessing market demand: Market research helps businesses to assess the demand for their products or services, enabling them to make informed decisions about pricing, distribution, and marketing strategies.

5.Developing a targeted marketing plan: Market research helps businesses to develop a targeted marketing plan that is tailored to the needs and preferences of their target customers, ensuring that marketing efforts are more effective and efficient.

In summary, conducting market research is a critical component of a successful business strategy. It helps businesses to gain a deeper understanding of their target customers, competitors, and the market in which they operate, enabling them to identify opportunities for growth and develop strategies that are tailored to their specific needs. By investing in market research, family businesses can make informed decisions about the future direction of their company, and position themselves for long-term success.

IDENTIFYING COMPETITIVE ADVANTAGES AND UNIQUE SELLING POINTS

Identifying competitive advantages and unique selling points is an essential process for any business seeking to differentiate itself from competitors and create value for its customers. A competitive advantage refers to any attribute or advantage that allows a business to outperform its rivals, while a unique selling point (USP) is a distinctive feature that sets a product or service apart from its competitors.

HERE ARE SOME KEY STEPS TO IDENTIFY COMPETITIVE ADVANTAGES AND UNIQUE SELLING POINTS

Understand Your Market: The first step in identifying competitive advantages and USPs is to understand your target market and their needs. Conduct market research to identify the key factors that influence customer buying decisions, including price, quality, convenience, and customer service.

Analyze Your Competitors: To differentiate your business from your competitors, you need to understand their strengths and weaknesses. Analyze their marketing strategies, pricing, product offerings, and customer experience to identify areas where you can differentiate yourself.

Identify Your Strengths: Conduct a SWOT analysis to identify your strengths, weaknesses, opportunities, and threats. Focus on your strengths and identify how you can leverage them to create value for your customers.

Determine Your Unique Value Proposition: Your unique value proposition (UVP) is the core message that communicates your competitive advantage and USP to your target audience. Your UVP should focus on what sets your business apart from competitors and why customers should choose you over other options.

Develop Your Brand Identity: Your brand identity is the way that customers perceive your business. It is important to create a consistent and compelling brand identity that reflects your competitive advantage and USP.

Test and Refine Your Message: Once you have identified your competitive advantage and USP, it is important to test your messaging with customers and refine it based on their feedback. This will help you to create a more effective marketing strategy and improve your customer experience.

In conclusion, identifying competitive advantages and unique selling points is a critical process for any business seeking to create value for its customers and stand out from competitors. By understanding your market, analyzing your competitors, and leveraging your strengths, you can develop a compelling UVP and brand identity that resonates with your target audience.

SETTING MEASURABLE GOALS AND OBJECTIVES

Setting measurable goals and objectives is an important step in achieving success in any area of life, including business, education, personal development, and more. Goals provide a clear direction and purpose, while objectives help to break down those goals into specific, measurable, achievable, relevant, and time-bound (SMART) steps.

Here are some key steps to setting measurable goals and objectives:

1.Define Your Goal: The first step in setting measurable goals and objectives is to define what you want to achieve. Your goal should be specific, clear, and actionable, such as increasing sales by 20% in the next quarter or completing a degree program within two years.

2.Identify Key Performance Indicators (KPIs): Key performance indicators are specific metrics that help you measure progress toward your goal. For example, if your goal is to increase sales, your KPIs might include the number of new leads generated, the conversion rate of those leads to customers, and the average order value.

3.Establish Baseline Metrics: Before you can measure progress, you need to establish a baseline metric. This is the current performance level of the KPI you are measuring. For example, if your current conversion rate is 5%, you will use that as your baseline metric.

4.Set Objectives: Objectives are specific, measurable steps that you will take to achieve your goal. These objectives should be SMART, meaning they are specific, measurable, achievable, relevant, and time-bound. For example, an objective to increase sales might be to generate 100 new leads per month or to increase the average order value by 10%.

5.Assign Responsibility and Accountability: To ensure that your objectives are achieved, it is important to assign responsibility and accountability. This means identifying who will be responsible for achieving each objective and setting up a system of accountability to ensure that progress is tracked and reported.

6.Monitor Progress: Regularly monitoring progress is important to ensure that you are on track to achieve your goals. This can be done through regular reporting and review meetings, where progress is discussed, and adjustments are made as needed.

7.Adjust Objectives as Needed: Sometimes, as you work toward your goal, you may need to adjust your objectives. This could be due to unforeseen circumstances or changes in the market. It is important to be flexible and make adjustments as needed to ensure that you stay on track to achieve your goal.

In conclusion, setting measurable goals and objectives is an important process for achieving success in any area of life. By defining your goal, identifying KPIs, establishing baseline metrics, setting SMART objectives, assigning responsibility and accountability, monitoring progress, and adjusting objectives as needed, you can achieve your desired outcomes and make progress toward your long-term goals.

DEVELOPING A PLAN FOR SUSTAINABLE GROWTH

Developing a plan for sustainable growth is an important process for businesses seeking to achieve long-term success while minimizing negative impacts on the environment, society, and economy. A sustainable growth plan should focus on creating value for all stakeholders, including customers, employees, investors, suppliers, and the community, while also reducing environmental impacts and promoting social responsibility.

HERE ARE SOME KEY STEPS TO DEVELOPING A PLAN FOR SUSTAINABLE GROWTH:

1.Define Your Vision and Values: The first step in developing a plan for sustainable growth is to define your vision and values. This means identifying what you want to achieve and what principles will guide your actions. This could include a commitment to social responsibility, environmental sustainability, and ethical business practices.

2.Conduct a Sustainability Assessment: A sustainability assessment is a process of evaluating your business practices and identifying areas where you can improve sustainability. This could include reducing energy and water consumption, minimizing waste and pollution, and promoting social responsibility.

3.Develop Sustainable Business Strategies: Based on the results of your sustainability assessment, develop sustainable business strategies that align with your vision and values. This could include using renewable energy sources, reducing packaging waste, and promoting fair labor practices.

4.Implement Sustainability Practices: Once you have developed sustainable business strategies, implement them across your organization. This may involve training employees on sustainable practices, investing in new technologies or processes, and partnering with suppliers who share your commitment to sustainability.

5.Monitor and Report Progress: To ensure that your sustainable growth plan is successful, it is important to monitor and report progress on a regular basis. This could involve tracking sustainability metrics, such as energy consumption and waste reduction, and reporting on progress to stakeholders.

6.Continuously Improve: Sustainable growth is an ongoing process, and it is important to continuously improve and refine your sustainability practices. This may involve setting new sustainability targets, investing in new technologies or processes, and engaging with stakeholders to identify new opportunities for improvement.

In conclusion, developing a plan for sustainable growth is an important process for businesses seeking to achieve long-term success while minimizing negative impacts on the environment, society, and economy. By defining your vision and values, conducting a sustainability assessment, developing sustainable business strategies, implementing sustainability practices, monitoring and reporting progress, and continuously improving, you can create value for all stakeholders while promoting environmental sustainability and social responsibility.

CHAPTER TWO

BUILDING A STRONG TEAM

Building a strong team is essential for any organization to achieve its goals and objectives. A team that works well together, communicates effectively, and collaborates on tasks can accomplish more than individuals working alone. A strong team can also increase employee engagement, job satisfaction, and retention, leading to improved performance and productivity. In this era of remote work and virtual teams, building a strong team requires a deliberate effort to create a culture of trust, openness, and collaboration, as well as providing the necessary tools and resources to support effective teamwork. In this article, we will explore some strategies and best practices for building a strong team in today's dynamic and rapidly changing workplace.

IMPORTANCE OF A STRONG TEAM

In today's competitive business world, the importance of having a strong team cannot be overstated. A strong team can bring tremendous benefits to an organization, including increased productivity, improved efficiency, and better decision-making. However, building a strong team is easier said than done. It requires careful planning, effective communication, and most importantly, hiring the right employees.

WHY IS A STRONG TEAM IMPORTANT?

A strong team is one in which all members work together towards a common goal, each bringing their own skills and strengths to the table. There are several reasons why a strong team is important for an organization:

1.Increased Productivity: When members of a team work well together, they can accomplish much more than they would as individuals. By leveraging each other's strengths and compensating for each other's weaknesses, team members can complete tasks more quickly and efficiently.

2.Improved Efficiency: A strong team is one in which each member understands their role and responsibilities. This clarity allows for a smoother workflow, fewer errors, and a reduction in wasted time and resources.

3.Better Decision-making: When a team is composed of individuals with diverse backgrounds, experiences, and perspectives, they are more likely to arrive at better decisions. This is because different perspectives can lead to a more comprehensive understanding of the problem at hand and a wider range of potential solutions.

4 Increased Morale: A strong team is one in which members feel valued and supported. When employees feel like they are part of a team that is working towards a common goal, they are more likely to be motivated and engaged in their work.

HIRING THE RIGHT EMPLOYEES

Building a strong team starts with hiring the right employees. Here are some tips to help you find the right people for your team:

1.Clearly Define the Role: Before you begin the hiring process, make sure you have a clear understanding of the role you are trying to fill. This will help you identify the skills and experience necessary for success in the role.

2.Look Beyond the Resume: While a candidate's resume can tell you a lot about their experience and qualifications, it's important to also consider other factors such as their personality, work style, and values. Look for candidates who are a good fit for your team culture and who share your organization's values.

3.Conduct Thorough Interviews: Conducting thorough interviews is essential to hiring the right employees. Ask questions that will help you understand the candidate's skills, experience, and work style. It's also important to ask behavioral questions that will give you insight into how the candidate handles challenging situations.

4.Check References: Checking references is an important step in the hiring process. Speak with the candidate's previous employers or colleagues to get a sense of their work style, strengths, and areas for improvement.

5.Emphasize Teamwork: During the hiring process, make it clear that teamwork is an important part of your organization's culture. Look for candidates who have a track record of working well with others and who value collaboration.

In conclusion, building a strong team is crucial for the success of any organization. By hiring the right employees and fostering a culture of teamwork and collaboration, you can create a team that is productive, efficient, and motivated.

Remember, a strong team is greater than the sum of its parts, and it is up to you as a leader to build and maintain a team that can achieve great things together.

CREATING A CULTURE OF EXCELLENCE

Creating a culture of excellence is an essential element for any organization seeking to achieve long-term success. A culture of excellence is defined as a work environment where everyone is committed to achieving the highest standards of quality, performance, and professionalism. In this article, we will explore some of the key elements of creating a culture of excellence and how organizations can achieve this.

1.Lead by Example: Creating a culture of excellence starts at the top. Leaders must embody the values and behaviors they want to see in their organization. They must model excellence in their work and inspire their team to strive for the same.

2.Hire the Right People: Building a team that is committed to excellence requires hiring people who share the same values and beliefs. When hiring new employees, look for individuals who are passionate about their work, have a track record of success, and are committed to continuous improvement.

3.Provide Ongoing Training and Development: To create a culture of excellence, it is essential to provide ongoing training and development opportunities to employees. This will help them develop their skills and stay up-to-date with the latest trends and best practices in their field.

4.Encourage Innovation: A culture of excellence is one that encourages innovation and creativity. Leaders should provide their team with the resources and support they need to develop new ideas and solutions.

5.Foster Open Communication: Creating a culture of excellence requires fostering open communication and feedback. Leaders should encourage their team to share their ideas, concerns, and feedback. This will help identify areas for improvement and promote a sense of ownership and accountability.

6.Recognize and Reward Excellence: Recognizing and rewarding excellence is an essential element of creating a culture of excellence. Celebrate the successes and accomplishments of your team and provide incentives for those who achieve exceptional results.

7.Emphasize Quality: In a culture of excellence, quality is a top priority. Leaders should emphasize the importance of quality in every aspect of their organization's work, from product development to customer service.

8.Maintain High Standards: To create a culture of excellence, it is essential to maintain high standards. Leaders should establish clear expectations for performance, conduct, and professionalism and hold their team accountable for meeting these standards.

In conclusion, creating a culture of excellence requires commitment, dedication, and ongoing effort. It is not something that can be achieved overnight, but rather a long-term goal that requires constant attention and nurturing. By leading by example, hiring the right people, providing ongoing training and development, fostering open communication, recognizing and rewarding excellence, emphasizing quality, and maintaining high standards, organizations can create a culture of excellence that will drive long-term success.

OFFERING COMPETITIVE SALARIES AND BENEFITS

Offering competitive salaries and benefits is a crucial component of any successful business. A competitive salary and benefits package helps attract and retain talented employees, which is essential for achieving long-term success. In this section, we will explore the benefits of offering competitive salaries and benefits, and how businesses can design a package that meets the needs of their employees.

1.Attract and Retain Talented Employees: A competitive salary and benefits package is essential for attracting and retaining talented employees. When employees feel valued and compensated fairly, they are more likely to stay with the company and contribute to its long-term success. On the other hand, if a company offers low salaries and benefits, talented employees are likely to leave for better opportunities.

2.Improve Employee Morale and Motivation: A competitive salary and benefits package can also improve employee morale and motivation. When employees feel they are compensated fairly for their work, they are more likely to feel motivated and engaged in their work. This can lead to increased productivity and better job performance.

3.Enhance Company Reputation: A company that offers competitive salaries and benefits is more likely to have a positive reputation in the industry. This can help attract top talent and create a positive image for the company.

4.Reduce Turnover and Recruitment Costs: High turnover and recruitment costs can be a significant expense for companies. By offering a competitive salary and benefits package, companies can reduce turnover rates and lower recruitment costs. This can help save time and money in the long run.

When designing a competitive salary and benefits package, companies should consider the following:

1.Conduct Market Research: Companies should conduct market research to determine the average salary and benefits packages offered by competitors in the industry. This can help ensure that the package offered is competitive and attractive to potential employees.

2.Determine the Needs of Employees:
Companies should consider the needs and
preferences of their employees when designing a
benefits package. This can include offering
health insurance, retirement plans, paid time off,
and other perks that are important to employees.

3.Consider the Budget: Companies should also
consider their budget when designing a benefits
package. While it is essential to offer
competitive salaries and benefits, companies
must also ensure that the package is financially
sustainable.

4.Communicate the Package to Employees:
Companies should communicate the benefits
package to employees clearly and transparently.
This can help build trust and confidence among
employees and ensure they understand the value
of their compensation package.

In conclusion, offering a competitive salary and
benefits package is essential for attracting and

retaining talented employees, improving morale and motivation, enhancing company reputation, and reducing turnover and recruitment costs. Companies that take the time to design a comprehensive and attractive package are more likely to succeed in the long run.

PROVIDING OPPORTUNITIES FOR TRAINING AND CAREER DEVELOPMENT

Providing Opportunities For training and career development is essential for both employees and employers. It helps employees to acquire new skills and knowledge, improve their job performance, and advance in their careers. At the same time, it helps employers to retain their top talent, increase productivity, and stay competitive in the market.

There are several ways in which organizations can provide training and career development opportunities for their employees. Some of them are:

1.On-the-job training: This type of training involves learning while doing. It can be done through job rotation, mentoring, coaching, and shadowing. On-the-job training allows employees to acquire new skills while working on real-world projects.

2.Classroom training: Classroom training involves attending seminars, workshops, and conferences. It provides employees with the opportunity to learn from experts in their field and network with other professionals.

3.Online training: Online training involves using digital platforms such as e-learning modules, webinars, and virtual classrooms. Online training is flexible, cost-effective, and can be done at the employee's own pace.

4.Job enrichment: Job enrichment involves giving employees more responsibilities, autonomy, and decision-making power. It allows employees to learn new skills and take on new challenges.

5.Tuition reimbursement: Tuition reimbursement involves the employer paying for an employee's education or training outside of work. This can include courses, certifications, or degree programs.

When providing training and career development opportunities, it's important to consider the needs and goals of each employee. Some employees may want to advance in their current role, while others may want to switch to a different role or department. Employers can work with their employees to create individualized career development plans that align with their career goals.

In conclusion, providing opportunities for training and career development is crucial for the growth and success of both employees and employers. It helps employees to acquire new skills, improve their job performance, and advance in their careers. At the same time, it helps employers to retain their top talent, increase productivity, and stay competitive in the market.

ENCOURAGING OPEN COMMUNICATION AND COLLABORATION

Encouraging open communication and collaboration is essential for building a positive and productive workplace culture. When employees feel comfortable sharing their thoughts and ideas, they are more likely to work together to achieve common goals, solve problems, and innovate. Here are some ways to promote open communication and collaboration in the workplace:

1.Foster a culture of respect: The foundation of open communication and collaboration is mutual respect. Employers can create a culture of respect by setting clear expectations for how employees should treat one another, modeling respectful behavior, and addressing any disrespectful behavior that arises.

2.Encourage feedback: Encouraging employees to give feedback can help to identify areas for improvement and promote ongoing communication. Employers can do this by creating feedback channels, such as regular one-on-one meetings or anonymous suggestion boxes, and being responsive to employee feedback.

3.Facilitate team building activities: Team building activities can help to build trust and foster collaboration among employees. Activities can range from simple icebreakers to more complex team challenges, depending on the needs and preferences of the team.

4.Promote diversity and inclusion: A diverse and inclusive workplace encourages employees to share their unique perspectives and ideas, leading to more innovative and effective solutions. Employers can promote diversity and inclusion by creating a welcoming and supportive environment, providing diversity training, and actively recruiting a diverse workforce.

5.Use technology to facilitate communication: Technology can be a powerful tool for facilitating communication and collaboration, especially for remote or distributed teams. Employers can use tools such as video conferencing, instant messaging, and project management software to connect employees and streamline communication.

In conclusion, encouraging open communication and collaboration is critical for building a positive and productive workplace culture. Employers can foster a culture of respect, encourage feedback, facilitate team building activities, promote diversity and inclusion, and use technology to facilitate communication to achieve this goal.

CHAPTER THREE

ESTABLISHING CLEAR ROLES AND RESPONSIBILITIES

Establishing Clear roles and responsibilities is crucial in any organization or team to ensure that everyone knows what is expected of them and how they contribute to the overall success of the group. This involves defining and communicating each individual's specific duties, tasks, and functions, as well as their level of authority, accountability, and decision-making power. Clear roles and responsibilities can help prevent confusion, misunderstandings, and conflicts that may arise when people are unsure of what they should be doing or who is responsible for certain outcomes. It can also foster a sense of ownership, motivation, and collaboration among team members by promoting transparency, clarity, and fairness in the distribution of workload and recognition of achievements. Ultimately, establishing clear roles and responsibilities can contribute to achieving organizational goals and objectives, improving productivity, and building trust and respect within the team.

IMPORTANCE OF CLEAR ROLES AND RESPONSIBILITIES

Establishing clear roles and responsibilities is vital for the success of any organization or team. Here are some reasons why:

1.Avoid confusion and misunderstandings: Clearly defined roles and responsibilities help to prevent confusion and misunderstandings about what each team member is responsible for. When everyone understands their role, it's easier to avoid overlap, duplication, and gaps in responsibilities, which can lead to frustration, delays, and errors.

2.Increase accountability: When team members know exactly what they are responsible for, it's easier to hold them accountable for their performance. Clear roles and responsibilities also make it easier to track progress and measure outcomes, which helps to identify and address performance issues more effectively.

3.Improve communication and collaboration: Establishing clear roles and responsibilities promotes communication and collaboration among team members. When everyone knows what they need to do, they can work together more efficiently and effectively. It also helps to identify areas where collaboration is necessary and fosters a sense of teamwork and trust.

4.Enhance productivity: Clear roles and responsibilities ensure that each team member is working on tasks that align with their skills and expertise. This helps to increase productivity as team members can focus on what they do best and avoid wasting time on tasks outside their scope.

5.Facilitate decision-making: Clearly defined roles and responsibilities make it easier to make decisions as everyone knows who has the authority to make decisions on specific issues. This helps to avoid conflicts and ensures that decisions are made efficiently and effectively.

In summary, establishing clear roles and responsibilities is crucial for any organization or team. It helps to avoid confusion, increase accountability, improve communication and collaboration, enhance productivity, and facilitate decision-making.

DEFINING JOB DESCRIPTIONS

A job description is a written document that outlines the duties, responsibilities, and requirements of a specific job position within an organization. It serves as a guide for both employers and employees to understand the nature of the job and the skills and qualifications needed to perform it.

The process of defining job descriptions typically involves the following steps:

1.Identifying the need for a new job position or a revision of an existing one.

2.Conducting a job analysis to identify the essential duties, responsibilities, and skills required for the job.

3.Drafting a job description that includes the job title, summary of the position, essential functions and responsibilities, minimum qualifications and requirements, and any physical demands or working conditions.

4.Reviewing the job description with relevant stakeholders, such as the hiring manager, HR department, and current employees, to ensure accuracy and completeness.
Posting the job description in job ads and other relevant platforms to attract potential candidates.
Job descriptions serve several purposes, including:

5.Recruitment and selection: Job descriptions provide a clear understanding of the job position and its requirements, which can help attract qualified candidates and streamline the hiring process.

6.Performance management: Job descriptions establish clear expectations and goals for the job position, which can be used to evaluate employee performance and identify areas for improvement.

7.Career development: Job descriptions can be used as a basis for developing career paths and training programs for employees.

8.Compliance: Job descriptions can ensure compliance with legal and regulatory requirements, such as the Americans with Disabilities Act (ADA) and the Fair Labor Standards Act (FLSA).

In summary, defining job descriptions is a critical aspect of human resource management that helps organizations attract qualified candidates, establish clear expectations for employees, and ensure compliance with legal and regulatory requirements.

ASSIGNING SPECIFIC RESPONSIBILITIES TO EACH EMPLOYEE

Assigning specific responsibilities to each employee is an essential aspect of effective management in any organization. It involves identifying the unique skills, strengths, and expertise of each employee and allocating tasks and duties that match their abilities and interests.

HERE ARE SOME BENEFITS OF ASSIGNING SPECIFIC RESPONSIBILITIES TO EACH EMPLOYEE:

Improved productivity: When employees are assigned tasks that match their skills and experience, they are more likely to be productive and produce high-quality work. They are also more likely to take ownership of their work and be invested in its success.

1.Better accountability: Assigning specific responsibilities makes it clear who is responsible for each task or project, which increases accountability. Employees are more likely to take ownership of their work and take pride in their accomplishments when they have specific responsibilities.

2.Reduced conflicts: When employees have clear responsibilities, there is less room for misunderstandings and conflicts. Everyone knows what they are responsible for, and there is less overlap or ambiguity in roles.

3.Improved job satisfaction: When employees are assigned tasks that match their skills and interests, they are more likely to be satisfied with their job. This can lead to increased motivation and engagement, which can improve overall productivity.

4.Efficient use of resources: Assigning specific responsibilities ensures that resources, such as time and money, are used efficiently. When employees are assigned tasks that match their skills, they are more likely to complete them quickly and accurately, which can save time and reduce costs.

In summary, assigning specific responsibilities to each employee is essential for effective management and can lead to improved productivity, accountability, job satisfaction, reduced conflicts, and efficient use of resources.

DEFINING THE REPORTING STRUCTURE AND DECISION-MAKING PROCESS

Defining the reporting structure and decision-making process is crucial for any organization to function effectively. It involves determining the hierarchy of positions and departments within the organization, as well as outlining how decisions are made and communicated.

Here are some reasons why defining the reporting structure and decision-making process is important:

1.Clearly defined roles and responsibilities: Defining the reporting structure and decision-making process ensures that each employee understands their role and responsibilities within the organization. This helps to avoid confusion, duplication of efforts, and conflicts.

2.Efficient communication: When there is a clear reporting structure, communication channels are established and employees know who to go to for information or direction. This can lead to more efficient communication, faster decision-making, and increased productivity.

3.Effective decision-making: A well-defined decision-making process ensures that decisions are made in a consistent and transparent manner. This helps to avoid bias or favoritism and promotes accountability.

4.Better alignment with goals and objectives: When there is a clear reporting structure and decision-making process, decisions are aligned with the organization's goals and objectives. This helps to ensure that resources are used effectively and that everyone is working towards the same objectives.

5.Improved organizational culture: A well-defined reporting structure and decision-making process can contribute to a positive organizational culture. When employees know that decisions are made fairly and transparently, they are more likely to feel valued and motivated.

In summary, defining the reporting structure and decision-making process is critical for any organization to function effectively. It helps to ensure that roles and responsibilities are clear, communication is efficient, decisions are made effectively, goals are aligned, and the organizational culture is positive.

ESTABLISHING CLEAR LINES OF COMMUNICATION

Establishing clear lines of communication is crucial for any organization to function effectively. It involves creating channels for information to flow within and between departments, as well as establishing guidelines for how communication should occur.

HERE ARE SOME REASONS WHY ESTABLISHING CLEAR LINES OF COMMUNICATION IS IMPORTANT

Improved collaboration: When communication is clear and efficient, it facilitates collaboration between departments and individuals. This can lead to better problem-solving and decision-making.

1.Increased efficiency: When communication is clear, employees spend less time trying to figure out what they need to do or how to do it. This can lead to increased productivity and efficiency.

2.Improved morale: When employees feel like they have access to the information they need and can communicate effectively with their colleagues, they are more likely to feel valued and motivated.

3.Better customer service: When communication is clear, it is easier to respond to customer inquiries and resolve issues. This can lead to increased customer satisfaction and loyalty.

4.Reduced errors: When communication is clear, there is less room for misunderstandings or misinterpretations. This can reduce errors and mistakes in the workplace.

Establishing clear lines of communication can be achieved through a variety of methods, such as regular team meetings, clear and concise email communication, online collaboration tools, and open-door policies. It is important to establish guidelines for how communication should occur, such as the use of specific channels for certain types of communication, response times for emails, and expectations for professional and respectful communication.

In summary, establishing clear lines of communication is critical for any organization to function effectively. It can lead to improved collaboration, increased efficiency, improved morale, better customer service, and reduced errors. It requires establishing guidelines for communication and using a variety of tools and methods to facilitate clear and efficient communication within and between departments.

CHAPTER FOUR
EMBRACING TECHNOLOGY

embracing technology is a crucial aspect of success for any organization in today's world. Technology has rapidly transformed the way we live and work, and businesses that fail to adapt risk being left behind. By embracing technology, organizations can leverage new tools and innovations to increase efficiency, productivity, and profitability.

Technology has the potential to transform many aspects of a business, including communication, operations, marketing, and customer service. From cloud computing and automation to artificial intelligence and big data analytics, technology has created new opportunities for businesses to streamline processes, improve decision-making, and gain a competitive edge.

However, embracing technology also requires careful planning and management. It is important to assess the specific needs and goals of the organization, and to identify the most effective technologies to achieve those goals. It also requires training and support for employees to effectively use new technologies and adapt to changes in the workplace.

Overall, embracing technology is essential for organizations to remain competitive and successful in today's digital landscape. By leveraging new tools and innovations, businesses can improve efficiency, streamline processes, and better serve their customers. However, it also requires careful planning and management to ensure that technology is effectively integrated into the organization and aligned with its goals and values.

IMPORTANCE OF EMBRACING TECHNOLOGY

Technology has become an integral part of our lives, from our homes to our workplaces, and even to our personal relationships. Embracing technology is crucial in today's fast-paced and rapidly changing world, as it offers numerous benefits that improve the quality of our lives.

One of the most significant benefits of embracing technology is that it enhances efficiency and productivity. For instance, using a computer, mobile phone, or tablet can help people accomplish tasks faster and more efficiently than they could with traditional methods. This increased efficiency can lead to better job performance, which can improve job satisfaction and financial security.

Technology also provides people with more access to information and resources than ever before. The internet and other digital platforms have made it possible for people to connect with others, access educational resources, and stay informed on current events in real-time. This access to information can lead to more informed decision-making and improved overall knowledge and understanding.

Embracing technology can also help individuals stay connected with family and friends. Social media platforms and messaging applications allow people to communicate with loved ones no matter where they are in the world. These connections can help improve social and emotional well-being, particularly during times of isolation or loneliness.

In addition to personal benefits, embracing technology can also have significant impacts on the environment. Technologies like renewable energy and electric vehicles have the potential to reduce carbon emissions and mitigate the effects of climate change. Additionally, digital communication and remote work options can help reduce the need for commuting, thereby reducing traffic congestion and air pollution.

Finally, embracing technology can help individuals stay competitive in today's job market. As more industries become digitized, individuals who are comfortable with technology and can adapt to new technologies are more likely to be successful in their careers.

In conclusion, embracing technology is critical in today's world. The benefits it provides, from increased efficiency and productivity to better access to information and resources, make it an essential component of our lives. By embracing technology, individuals can improve their overall well-being, stay connected with others, and stay competitive in their careers.

IMPROVING EFFICIENCY AND PRODUCTIVITY

Efficiency and productivity are essential aspects of any successful organization. Improving these two factors can help a business reduce costs, increase profits, and gain a competitive advantage. Here are some strategies that can be used to improve efficiency and productivity:

1.Streamline Processes: Review and analyze existing workflows and processes to identify inefficiencies and bottlenecks. Simplify and streamline these processes by automating repetitive tasks and eliminating unnecessary steps. This can help reduce the time and effort required to complete tasks, which ultimately increases productivity.

2.Use Technology: Leverage technology tools and software to automate tasks and improve workflow. For example, project management software can help teams collaborate more effectively and manage tasks and deadlines more efficiently. Similarly, automated data entry tools can reduce the time and errors associated with manual data entry.

3.Provide Training: Investing in training and development can help employees acquire the skills and knowledge they need to perform their jobs more efficiently. Training can also help employees stay up-to-date with the latest technology and best practices, which can help improve productivity.

4.Set Goals and Track Progress: Set specific goals for employees and teams, and track progress regularly. This helps to ensure that everyone is working towards the same objectives and that progress is being made towards achieving those goals. Regular progress tracking also enables organizations to identify areas for improvement and adjust strategies as needed.

5.Prioritize Time Management: Time management is a critical factor in improving efficiency and productivity. Encourage employees to prioritize their time and focus on high-priority tasks first. Provide tools and resources, such as time management apps or project management software, to help employees manage their time more effectively.

6.Foster a Positive Work Environment: A positive work environment can help improve employee engagement, motivation, and productivity. Encourage collaboration and open communication, and recognize and reward employees for their contributions. This can help create a sense of ownership and pride in their work, which can lead to increased productivity and efficiency.

In conclusion, improving efficiency and productivity is essential for any organization looking to gain a competitive advantage. By streamlining processes, using technology, providing training, setting goals, prioritizing time management, and fostering a positive work environment, organizations can improve their overall efficiency and productivity, resulting in better outcomes and increased success.

ENHANCING CUSTOMER EXPERIENCE

Enhancing customer experience is a critical factor for businesses of all sizes and industries to succeed in today's competitive market. Customer experience refers to the overall perception a customer has of your brand based on their interactions with your products, services, and employees. A positive customer experience can lead to increased loyalty, repeat business, and positive word-of-mouth marketing.

HERE ARE SOME WAYS TO ENHANCE CUSTOMER EXPERIENCE:

1.Personalization: Customers appreciate a personalized experience. By understanding their preferences and behavior, businesses can offer personalized recommendations, discounts, and content. This approach can increase customer satisfaction and loyalty.

2.Responsiveness: Customers expect quick and efficient service. By providing prompt responses to inquiries and complaints, businesses can build trust and improve customer experience. This can be achieved through multiple channels such as email, phone, chat, and social media.

3.Consistency: Consistency in service delivery and product quality is crucial in building customer trust and loyalty. By maintaining consistency across all touchpoints, businesses can establish a reputation for reliability and dependability.

4.Ease of Use: Customers prefer simple and easy-to-use products and services. By eliminating unnecessary complexity and streamlining processes, businesses can make it easier for customers to engage with their brand.

5.Empathy: Showing empathy towards customers can go a long way in building a positive customer experience. By understanding their needs and concerns, businesses can provide tailored solutions that meet their expectations.

6.Continuous Improvement: To enhance customer experience, businesses need to be open to feedback and continuously improve their products and services. By soliciting feedback from customers and implementing changes based on their input, businesses can demonstrate their commitment to providing the best possible customer experience.

In conclusion, enhancing customer experience is critical to business success. By implementing strategies such as personalization, responsiveness, consistency, ease of use, empathy, and continuous improvement, businesses can differentiate themselves from the competition and build long-term customer loyalty.

STREAMLINING COMMUNICATION AND COLLABORATION

Effective communication and collaboration are essential components for the success of any organization. In today's fast-paced business environment, it is essential to streamline communication and collaboration to improve efficiency, productivity, and overall performance. Here are some ways to streamline communication and collaboration:

1.Use Collaborative Tools: There are various tools available for organizations to facilitate communication and collaboration, such as project management tools, instant messaging, and video conferencing tools. These tools can help teams work more effectively, share information quickly, and stay on track with project timelines.

2.Establish Clear Communication Guidelines: Clear communication guidelines should be established to ensure that everyone in the organization is aware of expectations around communication. Guidelines should include guidelines around channels for communication, response times, and escalation procedures.

3.Encourage Open Communication: Encouraging open communication is essential to streamline communication and collaboration. Managers and team leaders should create a culture of openness where employees feel comfortable expressing their opinions, ideas, and concerns.

4.Simplify Workflows: Streamlining workflows can help organizations reduce bottlenecks and improve productivity. This can be achieved by using automation tools to simplify repetitive tasks and eliminate the need for manual input.

5.Set Clear Objectives: Setting clear objectives can help teams stay focused on the task at hand and work more collaboratively. Objectives should be specific, measurable, achievable, relevant, and time-bound (SMART).

6.Foster a Collaborative Environment: Collaboration is more than just communication. It requires a culture of trust and respect, where employees are willing to share knowledge, resources, and expertise. Managers should create an environment that fosters collaboration by recognizing team contributions, providing opportunities for growth, and promoting a team-oriented mindset.

In conclusion, streamlining communication and collaboration is crucial for organizations to succeed in today's fast-paced business environment. By using collaborative tools, establishing clear communication guidelines, encouraging open communication, simplifying workflows, setting clear objectives, and fostering a collaborative environment, organizations can improve efficiency, productivity, and overall performance.

PROVIDING VALUABLE DATA INSIGHTS FOR INFORMED DECISION-MAKING

In today's data-driven world, organizations need to make informed decisions based on data insights. By providing valuable data insights, businesses can gain a competitive advantage, optimize performance, and drive growth. Here are some ways to provide valuable data insights for informed decision-making:

1.Identify Key Performance Indicators (KPIs): Key performance indicators are metrics that organizations use to track progress and measure success. By identifying and tracking KPIs, businesses can gain valuable insights into their performance and make data-driven decisions.

2.Use Data Visualization Tools: Data visualization tools help to simplify complex data sets and make them easier to understand. By presenting data in an easily digestible format, businesses can make data-driven decisions more efficiently.

3.Utilize Predictive Analytics: Predictive analytics uses historical data to identify patterns and predict future trends. By using predictive analytics, organizations can make informed decisions and take proactive measures to optimize performance.

4.Develop a Data-Driven Culture: Organizations should develop a data-driven culture where employees are encouraged to use data to inform decision-making. This can be achieved by providing training and resources to employees, incentivizing data-driven decision-making, and promoting data literacy.

5.Monitor and Measure Results: To ensure that data insights are providing value, organizations should monitor and measure results regularly. This will help to identify areas for improvement and fine-tune decision-making processes.

CHOOSING THE RIGHT TECHNOLOGY SOLUTIONS

Choosing the right technology solutions is crucial for businesses of all sizes and industries. Technology solutions can help organizations optimize performance, increase efficiency, and gain a competitive advantage. Here are some key factors to consider when choosing the right technology solutions:

1.Identify Business Goals and Objectives: Before selecting technology solutions, businesses should identify their goals and objectives. This will help to determine which technology solutions align with their strategic vision and provide the most value.

2.Assess Current Technology Infrastructure: It is essential to assess the current technology infrastructure to identify any gaps or limitations. This will help to determine which technology solutions can integrate with existing systems and provide the most significant impact.

3.Consider Scalability: As businesses grow, technology requirements change. When choosing technology solutions, it is important to consider scalability to ensure that the solutions can accommodate growth and evolving needs.

4.Evaluate Ease of Use: Technology solutions should be user-friendly and easy to use. This will help to increase adoption rates and reduce training costs.

5.Evaluate Security: Security should be a top priority when choosing technology solutions. Organizations should assess the security features of the technology solutions to ensure that sensitive data is protected.

6.Consider Total Cost of Ownership (TCO): TCO includes the initial cost of technology solutions, ongoing maintenance, and training costs. Organizations should evaluate TCO to determine the overall cost of technology solutions and ensure that they align with their budget.

7.Evaluate Customer Support: Technology solutions should come with reliable customer support. This will help to address any technical issues or concerns quickly and efficiently.

In conclusion, choosing the right technology solutions is essential for business success. By considering factors such as business goals and objectives, current technology infrastructure, scalability, ease of use, security, TCO, and customer support, organizations can select technology solutions that align with their strategic vision, provide the most value, and drive growth.

PROVIDING TRAINING AND SUPPORT FOR EMPLOYEES

Providing training and support for employees is crucial for business success. Well-trained and supported employees are more productive, efficient, and engaged. Here are some ways to provide training and support for employees:

1.Identify Training Needs: Before providing training, organizations should identify training needs. This will help to ensure that employees receive relevant and useful training that aligns with their roles and responsibilities.

2.Develop a Training Program: Once training needs have been identified, organizations should develop a training program. The training program should be designed to provide employees with the necessary skills, knowledge, and tools to perform their job duties effectively.

3.Provide Onboarding: Onboarding is an essential part of training and support for new employees. It helps to ensure that new employees feel welcome, understand the company culture, and have the necessary information to perform their job duties.

4.Use Multiple Training Methods: To ensure that employees receive training that meets their learning needs, organizations should use multiple training methods, including online training, classroom training, and on-the-job training.

5.Provide Ongoing Support: Ongoing support is essential to ensure that employees continue to develop their skills and knowledge. This can be achieved through coaching, mentoring, and continuing education opportunities.

6.Encourage Feedback: Encouraging feedback from employees is crucial to ensure that training and support meet their needs. Organizations should regularly solicit feedback from employees and use it to improve training and support programs.

7.Utilize Technology: Technology can be used to provide training and support to employees efficiently. Online learning platforms, virtual training sessions, and digital resources can be used to provide training and support to employees, regardless of their location.

In conclusion, providing training and support for employees is essential for business success. By identifying training needs, developing a training program, providing onboarding, using multiple training methods, providing ongoing support, encouraging feedback, and utilizing technology, organizations can ensure that employees have the skills, knowledge, and tools necessary to perform their job duties effectively. This will increase productivity, efficiency, and engagement, and drive business success.

CHAPTER FIVE

A SUCCESSION PLAN

A succession plan is a crucial component of any organization's long-term strategy. It outlines the process for transferring leadership roles and responsibilities to new leaders, ensuring continuity and stability. Succession planning helps organizations identify and develop internal talent, which reduces the risk of losing valuable knowledge and skills when key employees leave the organization. A well-designed succession plan also helps organizations respond to unexpected events such as retirements, resignations, and other personnel changes. This enables organizations to be proactive in identifying and preparing the next generation of leaders, ensuring that the organization can continue to thrive in the face of challenges and opportunities.

THE IMPORTANCE OF SUCCESSION PLANNING

Succession planning is a critical process that helps organizations prepare for the future by identifying and developing internal talent to fill key leadership roles. Here are some reasons why succession planning is essential for organizational success:

1.Ensures Continuity: Succession planning ensures that there is a smooth transition of leadership, minimizing disruption to the organization's operations. It ensures that the organization can continue to function effectively, even when key leaders leave.

2.Identifies and Develops Internal Talent: Succession planning helps organizations identify and develop internal talent. By providing employees with opportunities for growth and development, organizations can improve employee engagement and retention.

3.Reduces Risk: Succession planning reduces the risk of losing valuable knowledge and skills when key employees leave the organization. It helps to ensure that critical information is passed down to new leaders, minimizing the impact of turnover.

4.Increases Agility: Succession planning makes organizations more agile by enabling them to respond quickly to unexpected events. It ensures that there are individuals ready to step into key leadership roles, reducing the time it takes to fill critical positions.

5.Improves Performance: Succession planning can improve organizational performance by ensuring that there is a clear understanding of the skills, knowledge, and experience required for key leadership roles. It helps to ensure that the right people are in the right positions, maximizing performance and productivity.

6.Supports Long-Term Strategy: Succession planning is essential for achieving long-term strategic goals. It ensures that the organization has the leadership it needs to execute its strategy effectively and achieve its goals.

In conclusion, succession planning is essential for organizational success. It ensures continuity, identifies and develops internal talent, reduces risk, increases agility, improves performance, and supports long-term strategy. By investing in succession planning, organizations can ensure that they have the leadership they need to thrive in a constantly changing environment.

IDENTIFYING POTENTIAL SUCCESSORS

Identifying potential successors is a crucial part of the succession planning process. Organizations need to identify individuals who have the necessary skills, experience, and potential to fill key leadership roles in the future. Here are some ways to identify potential successors:

1.Identify Key Positions: The first step in identifying potential successors is to identify key positions that require succession planning. These positions may include executive-level roles or positions critical to the organization's operations.

2.Assess Current Employees: Once key positions have been identified, organizations should assess current employees' skills, experience, and potential to fill these positions. This can be done through performance evaluations, assessments, and feedback from supervisors and colleagues.

3.Look for High-Potential Employees: High-potential employees are individuals who have the potential to take on leadership roles in the future. These employees may demonstrate strong leadership skills, a willingness to learn and grow, and the ability to work effectively with others.

4.Develop a Talent Pipeline: Organizations can develop a talent pipeline by identifying employees who are not yet ready for key leadership roles but have the potential to develop the necessary skills and experience over time. These employees can be given opportunities for growth and development to prepare them for future leadership roles.

5.Consider External Candidates: Organizations may also consider external candidates when identifying potential successors. External candidates may bring new perspectives and experiences to the organization, and they can be a valuable addition to the talent pipeline.

6.Monitor Industry Trends: Organizations should monitor industry trends to identify emerging talent that could fill key leadership roles in the future. This can include attending industry events, networking with peers, and staying up-to-date with industry news and developments.

In conclusion, identifying potential successors is a crucial part of the succession planning process. By identifying key positions, assessing current employees, looking for high-potential employees, developing a talent pipeline, considering external candidates, and monitoring industry trends, organizations can ensure that they have the leadership they need to succeed in the future.

DEVELOPING A LEADERSHIP DEVELOPMENT PROGRAM

Developing a leadership development program is an important step for any organization that wants to cultivate and develop effective leaders. A leadership development program is a set of initiatives, activities, and resources designed to enhance the leadership skills and abilities of individuals within the organization.

HERE ARE SOME STEPS TO CONSIDER WHEN DEVELOPING A LEADERSHIP DEVELOPMENt PROGRAM:

1.Define the Purpose and Objectives: The first step is to define the purpose and objectives of the program. This involves identifying the leadership competencies that are required for success in the organization, such as strategic thinking, communication, decision-making, and team building.

2.Conduct a Needs Assessment: A needs assessment helps to identify the areas where leadership development is most needed. This involves gathering data through surveys, interviews, focus groups, and other methods to determine the current state of leadership within the organization, the skills and abilities that need improvement, and the goals of the program.

3.Create a Development Plan: Based on the needs assessment, a development plan should be created that outlines the strategies and activities to be used to improve leadership skills. This may include coaching, mentoring, training, job shadowing, and other methods.

4.Develop the Program: With the development plan in place, the program can be created. This involves creating materials and resources, such as training manuals, online courses, and other resources, as well as identifying trainers and facilitators who will deliver the program.

5.Implement the Program: Once the program is developed, it should be implemented according to the development plan. This may involve scheduling training sessions, assigning mentors or coaches, and monitoring progress.

6.Evaluate the Program: Finally, the program should be evaluated to determine its effectiveness. This may involve gathering feedback from participants, assessing changes in leadership behavior and performance, and measuring the impact of the program on the organization.

Developing a leadership development program is an ongoing process, and it requires commitment and resources from the organization. However, a well-designed and implemented program can help to improve leadership skills, enhance organizational performance, and support the long-term success of the organization.

ESTABLISHING A GOVERNANCE STRUCTURE

Establishing a governance structure typically involves defining the rules, processes, and procedures by which an organization is run, managed, and controlled. The governance structure can help ensure that the organization's goals and objectives are aligned with its values and mission, and that it operates in a transparent, accountable, and efficient manner.

HERE ARE SOME STEPS TO CONSIDER WHEN ESTABLISHING A GOVERNANCE STRUCTURE:

1.Define the mission and objectives of the organization: This involves identifying the organization's purpose, vision, and values, as well as its short-term and long-term goals.

2.Identify the stakeholders: Stakeholders are individuals or groups who have an interest or influence in the organization's operations and outcomes. It is important to identify and prioritize stakeholders and understand their needs and expectations.

3.Determine the decision-making structure: This involves deciding who has the authority to make decisions, how decisions will be made, and what types of decisions require approval from higher levels.

4.Develop policies and procedures: Policies and procedures are the rules and guidelines that govern the organization's operations. These should be developed based on the organization's goals and objectives, and should be reviewed and updated regularly.

5.Establish roles and responsibilities: This involves defining the roles and responsibilities of key individuals and groups within the organization, such as the board of directors, executive team, and employees.

6.Establish communication channels: Communication is essential for effective governance. It is important to establish clear communication channels between stakeholders and to ensure that information is communicated in a timely and transparent manner.

7.Monitor and evaluate performance: Governance structures should include mechanisms for monitoring and evaluating performance against established goals and objectives, and for making adjustments as needed.

Establishing a governance structure can be a complex process that requires input and involvement from various stakeholders. It is important to approach this process with transparency, inclusivity, and a commitment to continuous improvement.

CONCLUSION

In conclusion, family businesses are a vital component of our global economy, and they come with their unique set of challenges and opportunities. Growing a family business requires careful planning, strong leadership, and a willingness to adapt to changing market conditions.

One of the most crucial factors in the growth of a family business is the ability to build and maintain strong family relationships. Family members must have a shared vision for the future of the business and must be able to work together towards common goals. Communication is key, and open and honest dialogue is critical to ensure that everyone is on the same page.

Another important aspect of family business growth is the need for professionalization. As the business grows, it becomes increasingly important to bring in outside expertise to help manage the business's complexities. This may involve hiring a CEO or other senior executives who are not family members, as well as implementing formal governance structures such as a board of directors.

Technology is also a critical factor in the growth of family businesses. Embracing technology can help family businesses stay competitive and efficient, whether through the use of digital marketing, e-commerce platforms, or cloud-based accounting software.

Finally, successful family businesses must be willing to adapt to changing market conditions. This means being flexible and agile, and constantly looking for new opportunities to innovate and grow. By staying true to their values and maintaining a focus on the long-term, family businesses can continue to thrive for generations to come.

In conclusion, while family businesses face unique challenges, there are many tips and strategies that can help them achieve sustainable growth. By fostering strong family relationships, professionalizing the business, embracing technology, and staying flexible and adaptable, family businesses can continue to thrive and remain a vital part of our global economy.

www.ingramcontent.com/pod-product-compliance
Lightning Source LLC
Chambersburg PA
CBHW071138220526
45467CB00015B/1460